CHALKDUST

Prayer Meditations of a Teacher

Elspeth Campbell Murphy

BAKER BOOK HOUSE
Grand Rapids, Michigan 49506

Published by Baker Books
a division of Baker Book House Company
P.O. Box 6287, Grand Rapids, MI 49516-6287

ISBN: 0-8010-6065-6

Twenty-sixth printing, February 1997

Printed in the United States of America

To my husband
Michael,
the finest teacher I've ever known,
and to the children
of Jonesville Elementary School,
Yemassee, South Carolina.

Contents

PART 1

Prayers for the Children

For the Child with a Bad Reputation

There's a little boy coming in the door, Father.
It's only the first day of school,
but I already know a lot about him.

From his records I know that
while his I.Q. is above average,
his "degree of consistency of effort on study assignments
has been unsatisfactory."
An underachiever.

I also know that he has "exhibited a lack of acceptance
of reasonable authority."
A discipline problem.

His reputation precedes him.
Even as he walks through the door,
I know all about him.

But, gracious Father,
in your lovingkindness you designed the perfect gift
for imperfect human beings: a fresh start.
And it is a gift you bestow
as often as we come to receive it.

Mistakes need not be cumulative;
each day can be a new beginning.
Father,
freely I have received;
now let me freely give.
There's a little boy coming in the door
who could use a fresh start.

For the Slow Learner

Oh, Father,
this child is so slow,
and I am so impatient.
We are both trying hard,
and I desperately need to see some success.

If only I could see a little progress—
slow, plodding progress.
But the word he read yesterday
he can't read today.
The math concept he seemed to grasp yesterday
has slipped away today.

And somewhere inside me
Discouragement is moaning, "Give up."

Help me not to listen.

Help me instead to listen for your voice
reminding me of all the good and true things
I've learned about teaching.

Remind me that progress is more a spiral staircase
than a straight flight of steps;
that learning rarely moves at a heartening pace;
it is more likely to dip and double back,
and move on in little spurts of growth.

So help me, Father,
not to give up when we move so slowly,
or stand still,
or even seem to slip backwards.
Give to me, and to this child,
the sure and steady faith to keep on trying.

But, Father,
when I grit my teeth and try so hard
that I am overcome with impatience,
let me hear your still, small voice saying,
"Relax!"

For the Handicapped Child

F ather,
she's just like all the other kids.

Except that she has
the longest, reddest hair
in the whole class.

Except that she got
a real, live German shepherd puppy
for her birthday,
and no one else in the whole class
has a dog like that.

Except that she can
say all of "The Night Before Christmas"
whenever anybody asks her to,
without ever getting stuck.

Except that the afternoon sun
slanting in the window
glints on the metal brace
clamped around her leg.

Except for all that,
she's just like all the other kids.

For the Very Bright Child

Father,
I don't have to plead for her attention
or devise tricks to keep it.
She eagerly takes in everything I have to teach her,
then goes off to learn more on her own.

I am delighted.

But I am also concerned,
for already I detect signs of arrogance in her.

Father,
with all her knowledge,
let her get understanding.
Keep her from assuming that intelligence
can take the place of compassion
or humor.

And as her teacher,
keep me from setting undue store by brilliance.
Let my classroom be both a relaxed
and an exciting place,
where each child—from the slowest learner to the
    gifted—
does the best he can,
where the challenge of learning
never overpowers the joy.

For the Troubled Child

Father,
I look into this little face that never smiles,
and I wonder what can be going on
behind those troubled eyes.

If I am impatient with her behavior,
it's because I don't understand it.
I'm bewildered.
And even a little frightened.

Oh, Father,
I fear that this world is a cold and hostile place
for some of these,
your children.
They seem preoccupied with troubles
they can't begin to understand.

As her teacher,
I feel at a loss to help this little girl.
I don't even know what's wrong.

Guide me, Father.
Show me my place in all of this.
Remind me daily
that this child is infinitely precious
in your sight.

And help this child
to believe that she matters to you,
because I've been able to show her
that she matters to me.

For the Child I Especially Like

He walks in,
and the room brightens a little.
He carries an aura of well-being and happiness
wherever he goes.
He greets the world openly,
reaching out with acceptance and warmth.
What a joy it is to teach a child
who is so well-balanced and unselfconscious;
who's disciplined, but not compulsive;
high-spirited, but not rowdy;
intelligent, but not arrogant.
Guide me, Father,
as I try to guide this young person
to whom so much has been given.
And thank you, Father,
for granting me the pleasure of his company.

For the Child I Don't Especially Like

Help me, Father.
I don't like this kid.
And I confess I'm inclined to pick on him.
He has a peculiar knack
for being in the wrong place at the wrong time,
and often he bears the blame
when I am mad at the world.
I seem to be after him for *every* little thing,
but, Father,
there are *so many* little things.
A more annoying child would be *very* hard to find.
He gets on my nerves,
and when I'm nervous,
I take it out on him.
It's a vicious circle.

Father, help me as I grapple
with these feelings of irritation and dislike.
Help me, at least, to be fair.
And then perhaps
fairness can lead to kindness,
and kindness to affection.

For the Quiet Child

The day began with more than the usual commotion,
and it was mid-morning
before I realized she wasn't there.

Forgive me, Lord.

Make me sensitive to your quiet ones,
for in a loud and pushy world
they are so often overlooked.

Make me sensitive.
Their silence may be hiding inner turmoil,
so let me be quick to see in their faces
those things which they cannot tell me in words.

Make me sensitive.
Keep me from thinking
that there is something innately wrong with silence,
that all children should be boisterously the same.
You have filled the world,
and my classroom,
with dazzling variety;
keep me from trying to homogenize it.

Help me to take notice of my shy students,
and to draw them out,
but without violating their freedom to be themselves.
Let me encourage them to stand up for their rights,
but keep me from violating their basic right to silence.

Lord, thank you for your quiet ones,
for in a loud and pushy world,
they are a calm oasis
and a balm for the soul.

For the Class Clown

There he goes—
an exuberant bundle of noise and laughter.
He doesn't walk, he bounces.
He doesn't talk, he whoops.
There he goes—
a little clown
dedicated to the proposition that life is hilarious.
His every action is an antic;
his every move a slapstick pantomime.

Father, I confess that
his sparkle,
his zest,
his *joie de vivre*,
doesn't rub off—
it just rubs.
Five minutes in his presence,
and I'm reduced to an exhausted, shrieking old crone.

Oh, Father, give me a little more patience.
Soothe my frayed nerves,
and restore my good humor.
Let this child teach me
to take delight in life,
even as I teach him
to take delight in moderation.

For the Rejected Child

You see her, Lord Jesus,
standing all alone on the edge of the playground.
A forlorn and funny little figure,
whose clothes are not quite right,
whose hair is not quite right,
whose speech is not quite right.

You see her, Lord.
A funny little figure standing alone,
because in the grim opinion of all the other ducklings,
she's not quite right.

What am I to do?
I can't force the other children to play with her.
That would only make matters worse,
would only turn a spotlight
on her pain.

I look at her standing there,
blink hard,
and look away.

Oh, Lord Jesus,
why do there have to be outcasts?
If I were in charge,
there'd be none of that;
we'd all be emphatically
equal.
No one would be cast aside
to suffer the pangs of loneliness
because of funny clothes
and funny hair
and funny speech.
We'd all be, well—
acceptable ducklings.

But I hear your firm rebuke.
I want acceptable ducklings;
You want glorious swans.
Your ways are not my ways.
You see the infinite value
of the weak,
the humble,
and even the funny-looking.
And who knows but that the pain of being different
might be your preparation
for greatness?

So give me some of your vision.
Help me to see the promise
in that lonely little girl.
Show me where her talents lie,
so that I can show them to her.
Let me give to her—
herself.

Thank you for reminding me
that there is no one
more loving than you,
no one more sensitive to the abandoned
and the lonely than you.
You—
who flung wide your arms of love
and gathered in the outcasts:
the half-breeds,
the lepers,
the prostitutes,
the maimed.

Oh, Lord Jesus,
open your arms a little wider,
and gather in that forlorn and funny little figure—
and me.

For the Child Who Lies and Steals

Oh, Father,
here we go again.

Caught red-handed,
he looks at me out of solemn eyes
and swears he's not to blame.

"Look," I say,
hating the earnest pomposity of my voice,
"It's bad enough to steal something;
it only makes matters worse
to lie about it."

And the quizzical frown on his face
seems genuine:
If you're caught stealing,
what else would you do but lie?

But it's the lying
that really gets to me, Father.
Time and again
I have looked searchingly into his face,
unable to tell whether "lie" or "truth"
was written there.

Time and again
he has broken trust,
making a mockery
of the benefit of the doubt.

And time and again
I have been tempted
to shrug
and let him go.

But, Father,
how can I let him go?

How can I not tell him
that it is wrong to lie and cheat and steal?

He's a moral infant, Father,
and sometimes I feel as though I'm raising him alone.
Surely I can't be the only one
who loves him enough to tell him, "No."

Oh, Father,
if I'm not the one who can reach him,
please send him someone who can.

For the Unmotivated Child

Lord, I'm exasperated!
He won't even try.
Children with far less natural ability
struggle on like determined little tortoises—
while the hare just sits,
his mind asleep.

Lord, I've tried so hard to rouse him.
I've prodded and threatened and cajoled.
And if there's some incentive I've overlooked,
some method I haven't tried,
please show me what it is.

But perhaps the time for prodding has passed.
Perhaps the time for decision is here.
And it is a decision only he can make:
to wake himself up
and run the race that is set before him.

Please let him make that decision, Lord,
before it is too late,
and he is left far, far behind.

For the New Child

Oh, I know,
it's hard to be the new kid.
But, Father, really.
The room is far too crowded as it is!
Where will I put another child?
And coming so late in the year—
when we're all so far along in math—
how he'll catch up, I just don't know.
And the reading program he was in
was totally different from this one.
And all the plants for the science project are coming up,
and we'll have to start his from scratch, and. . . .

Oh, Father,
there he stands
in the doorway,
with a brand-new red notebook
clutched at his side.

And the little hand
I hold in mine
when I introduce him to the class
is trembling.

He's not "another kid";
he's Tony.
"We're so glad to have you in our class, Tony,"
I hear myself saying.

And suddenly,
I mean it.

On the Forgiving Spirit of Children

Oh, Father, I get so discouraged sometimes.
I brood about how irritable and unreasonable I have
    been.
And I think, if I had been a kid in my class today,
would I want to come back tomorrow?

But tomorrow they are there,
and—miraculously—they are glad to see me.
Young children are the most forgiving people in your
    world, Father.
Even to seventy times seven.
And their generosity
is the antidote for my discouragement.
For they trust me enough
to let me start again.
And I love them enough
to want to try again.

Because of them
I glimpse your love
which bears all things,
believes all things,
hopes all things,
and endures all things.
Bless us, Father, as we follow your example
and forgive one another in love.

Jesus and the Children

Oh, Lord Jesus,
some days I wonder what you saw in them.

How could you gather those whiny, crabby little humans
in your arms
and bless them?
Did they push and shove to get to you,
or worse yet,
take cuts in line?
Did they tattle on their best friend
or ruthlessly tease the victim of the week?

That's the reality of kids, Lord.

Oh, but help me to remember
that no less real
is their curiosity, their open-heartedness, their zest.
Nowhere but in children
do we see such receptive, eager, and humble learners.

So, Lord Jesus,
remind me what you saw in them:
the very kingdom of heaven.

In Praise of Children

Lord, you have made these children
as varied as the flowers of a garden.
You have blessed each one uniquely.
And each fragile, growing child
is infinitely precious in your sight.
You have trusted me to nurture them.
And blessed me with the joy of seeing them grow.
Lord, I teach in reverence.

PART 2

Prayers for Special Times

On the Night Before School Starts

School starts tomorrow, Lord, and I'm nervous.
Ease my anxiety.
Give me confidence,
and let my confidence give the children security.

Let my external control
be a means of promoting their inner control,
so that classroom order
becomes a shared responsibility.

Let me have the kind of self-control
that teaches by example.

And let my discipline be patterned after yours,
rooted in a love
that will settle for nothing less than their best.

School starts tomorrow, Lord; make me ready.
You have given me a job to do
and the ability to do it well.
You have given me your promise that you will never
   leave me.
And you have guided me in all my preparation.

So now let me face tomorrow
eagerly and unafraid,
for ultimately my confidence rests in this:
"I am ready for anything
through the strength of the one
who lives within me" (Phil. 4:13, Phillips).

On the First Day of School

It's the first day of school, Lord,
the beginning of a school year as fresh
as the children's slick, unopened notebooks
and newly-sharpened pencils.

It's the first day of school,
and already I'm mentally exploring the new year,
wondering if I'll see the familiar landmarks
I've seen in years past.

Will September again be that rocky period of adjustment
when we must settle the question
of who's in charge here?

Will October again see routines well established
before the onset of Halloween hysteria?

Will November again see the class suddenly "jell"
and begin to function as a group?

Will Christmas again come all too quickly?

Will January see achievement levels spread far apart,
with some children off and flying,
and others barely started?

Will February ever end?

Will March produce another crop of late bloomers?

Will April bring my usual case of springtime regrets
and anxieties over work yet undone?

Will May bring the same restless euphoria?

Will June bring the same ambivalent feelings—
rejoicing at the arrival of summer,
yet regretting the departure of the children?

It's the first day of school, Lord,
and the year ahead seems reassuringly predictable.
But, while I guess at what this year might bring,
only you know what it will bring.
Only you know the future,
with all its problems
and joys.
God of all our days, I commit this year to you.

At the End of a Good Day

Father,
today I felt your presence
in the classroom.
By faith I know that you are always there,
but thank you for those times which *confirm*
that in you we live
and move
and have our being.

Father,
today it all felt so *right*.
The children were joyously absorbed
in what they were learning,
and I moved among them
full of the satisfaction of a job well done.
Thank you for those times of quiet joy
when it is good
just to be.
Thank you for gently reminding me
that you have brought the children and me together
for a purpose,
and that the work you have given me to do
is a sacred trust.

On a Rainy Day

"Is that any way to start the morning?"
I yell at the two children
I have just relegated to opposite ends of the room
for fighting.

Father, the first bell just rang,
and already this day has all the makings of a disaster.

The steady downpour of rain shows no sign
of letting up.
And, sensing that they will be indoors all day,
the children are busy practicing being restless and noisy.

The latest mandate from the office means one thing—
more paperwork.

Five children are trying to talk to me at once.

I shush them while I try to arrange the mounds
of miscellaneous paper on my desk into
neat mounds of miscellaneous paper.

The five children persist
and at last are able to communicate
that Sharon just threw up.
Somehow, I am not surprised.

Is this any way to start the morning?

Father, stop me.
Stop me from declaring this day a disaster
before it's even begun.

Save me from wasteful anxiety
over things I can't control,
and help me to work on something that only I can
    control—
my attitude.

Father, this is a day
that you have made.
Help me to rejoice and be glad in it.
This is a rainy day that you have made.
Help me to relax
and take it a little at a time.

In the Middle of a Bad Day

Father,
help me to recognize a bad day for what it is—
a day.
It does not represent the rest of the year,
or the rest of the month,
or even the rest of the week.
Keep me from making value judgments based on this
    day.
Keep me from deciding that the children are hopeless,
that my work is in vain,
and that I am a failure.

Oh, Father,
I'm discouraged and tired today,
but I'm not a failure.
I'm disorganized and frazzled today,
but the classroom still functions.
I'm impatient and crabby today,
but the children know I love them.

It's a bad day today,
but it's only a day.
It will pass.
Give me the patience to wait it out,
and to hold my letter of resignation
until tomorrow!

After Being "Pink-Slipped"

I got the news today, Father.
It's not as if I hadn't been expecting it;
I had.
It's just that
somewhere,
in the dimmest corners of my mind,
where hope lives,
I thought it might not happen.

I thought funds,
manna-like,
would suddenly appear.
Not ample funds,
but adequate.
Funds to buy materials,
continue programs,
hire us all back.

It's not as if it's final, though,
it's not.
The word is,
"wait-and-see."

Wait-and-see.
Can anything be harder?
I'd almost rather *know*.
And just by knowing
squelch the anxious hope
that I'll be back. . . .

But, oh, Father,
let me be back.
Yes, of course,
I need the money,
but it's more than that—

I need, well—
me.
I'm afraid that if I lose my job—
I'll lose myself.

Oh, Father,
bear me through this awful time
of despair and hope.
Give me the stamina
to wait-and-see,
the strength to face whatever comes.
And give me—me.

My job is what I *do*,
not what I am.
And what I am is—yours.
Your child.
Your trusting child.

At Grading Time

There they sit, Father,
a neat stack of yellow report cards.
And here I sit,
an anxious and bewildered Solomon,
praying in my heart for wisdom,
while the controversy about grading surges on.

Should there be an objective standard
whereby children are measured against other children?

And how do we weigh a child's achievement
against his ability and effort?
Can we penalize a child for having little natural ability,
when he can't get a high mark
no matter how hard he tries?
And what about the child for whom "A"s come easily?
Will he skim through school never knowing what it is to
   try?

And what is happening
when an "A" becomes so important that a child will
   cheat for it,
perhaps to avoid abuse at home?

So here I sit, Father,
forced to take these cards seriously
because other people do.
Long on questions,
short on answers.

Father,
as I reach reluctantly for the top card,
let me also reach for your promise:
"If any one of you lacks wisdom,
let him ask of God

who gives to all men generously
and without reproaching,
and it will be given him" (James 1:5).

During the Excitement of Holidays

F ather,
thank you for jack-o-lanterns
and brown sack turkeys,
for cotton-bearded Santas
and paper doily valentines.

Thank you for holidays,
and for the love of life
and renewal of creativity
which they inspire.

Thank you for children
and for their contagious sense of festival.
Father,
bless this day for them;
And for their teacher,
an extra measure of grace?

On the Day of the Field Trip

Father, we're going on a field trip this morning,
and I would ask that you . . .

Excuse me a minute, Father,
someone just said that the buses are here . . .

> All right, it's time to line up.
> Find your partners, please.

Have to count noses one more time, Father.

> All set? Then, let's go. Walk, Christopher.

Oh, Father, about Christopher,
please don't let him . . .

> All right, children.
> Please remember that your bus number is 120.
> That way, if you get separated from your group
> at the museum
> you'll be able to find the bus
> in the parking lot.
> Of course, you're not going to get separated
> from your group,
> but if you do,
> your bus number is 120.
> Now, let me hear you say it, 120.

Oh, Father,
please don't let me lose any of them.

> Christopher, put your name tag on, please.
> You absolutely must wear your name tag.

Let me catch my breath, Father.
They're all safely on the bus,
and we're ready to roll.

Scoot over, Christopher,
I'll sit beside you, I think.
Yes, yes. You can have the window.

Whew, Father.
Where was I?
Oh, yes.
Please help me to relax and have a good time.
I don't know why, but suddenly I remember a prayer
Sir Jacob Astley, the Puritan general,
once prayed:

"Lord, Thou knowest we must be busy today.
If we forget Thee,
do not Thou forget us."

Amen, Father,

Amen.

In the Middle of a Long, Dull Stretch

Father,
I confess that the prospect of another day
stretching before me
is a burden,
rather than a joy.

I've lived these past few weeks
in a state of mental and emotional malaise,
going routinely about my work,
without those sparks of creativity and spontaneity
that make life so exciting and satisfying.

The days are hectic,
crammed with pressures and demands,
but the hours pass slowly by—empty and barren.

Refresh me, Father.

Ease the tension that comes from boredom.

Show me how to bring vitality to a job that's gone stale.

Restore to me the absorbing joy of an artist at work,
for truly good teaching is an art.
Oh, Father,
you have given me time,
and you have given me skill.
Teach me to take delight in both,
using my time and my skill
to do something worthwhile,
to teach.

Before Being Evaluated

Well, Father, I *am* a little nervous,
but an hour from now
it will all be behind me.
An hour from now
I'll look back and smile.
And I'll think with relief,
"Well, that wasn't so bad!
The lesson went smoothly,
the kids were attentive,
the principal was impressed.
Not bad at all."
An hour from now
it will all be behind me.
An hour from now
I'll look back and smile.

I hope.

At the Teachers' Workshop

From theories and studies,
long-winded devotees,
and things that go clunk in the class,
Good Lord, deliver us.

After Losing My Temper

Oh, God,
he pushed me too far
this time—
right to the brink of my endurance.
But he didn't push me over
the brink;
I jumped.
Kicked my professional discretion aside
and jumped.

In the parlance of the trade,
I "overreacted."
Oh, God,
I let him have it.

And now,
sitting alone at my desk,
I hold a coffee cup in trembling hands
and wonder what will happen to me.
I fight down panic.
And the rage
that flares up
every time I think of that kid.
Oh, that kid!

And for every bit of rage I feel toward him,
I feel a double portion for myself;
how could I be so *stupid*?
And sinking down
through all my feelings,
settling like a rock,
is a little lump of shame.

Oh, Father,
I gather up my wretched little bundle

of anger, fear, and shame
and lay it at your feet.

After the Gripe Session

I don't know who said it, Father,
but it's true:
"Nothing unites a people like a mutual foe."
The fact that taking lunch room duty
is only a little like marching off to World War Two
is beside the point.
The unity is the important thing.

Oh, but it was exhilarating
out on the playground this morning, Father.
Exhilarating,
to put our petty differences aside,
join hands and hearts,
and raise our voices
in One Great Gripe.

The exhilarating unity!
The spirit of comradery!
The fun of the common cause!
It's the stuff of revolution!

To put our petty differences aside,
join hands and hearts,
and—

But then the recess bell rang, and
keyed up
wrung out
let down
we gathered our kids
and straggled back to our rooms
alone.

After Hearing That a Child's Parent Has Died

Father,
the principal was just here to give me the news.
Johnny's mother
just died in an automobile accident.
I only nodded when he told me.
Now I turn back to the room.

The children stare at me, knowing something is wrong—
terribly,
terribly
wrong.
I clear my throat,
"Get out your math books," I tell them.
"I'll write the page numbers on the board."
They do as they are told.

They listen to me, Father.
And soon I'll have to tell them.
They'll look at me, and listen,
but they will not understand.

And soon I'll have to talk to Johnny.
He listens to me, too.
I'll talk to him
and hope with all my being
that he doesn't ask me,
Why?

Because, oh, my God,
I cannot tell him
what I do not know.

On the Last Day of School

Father,
a quiet tension fills the room
on this last day of school.
I expected exuberance and rowdiness,
but that came yesterday,
when there was still one day to go.
Today the children are disturbingly subdued.
I am embarrassed at my own emotions;
I cannot look at the children directly.

The room is so blank.
Our desks are cleaned out.
The last traces of the party have been swept away.
The charts and posters are down for the summer.

So now we sit quietly,
too wrought even for songs and games,
and we wait for the bus to come.

I expect to see these children again, of course,
but it won't be the same.
They know it,
and I know it.

They will come around to see me,
jealous of the new class,
and I will look at a room of little strangers
and miss the familiar faces.

In time
the strangers will become friends.
But every class is different and special;
no new group of children will ever take the place
of the one leaving me today.

Lord,
I have worked hard,
and I have loved these children dearly.
In investing in their future
I have cast my bread upon the waters,
content that I will find it after many days.

Lord, I commend them into your hands.

PART 3

Prayers for the Teacher

For Renewal

Oh, Father!
The fights over who took whose pencil,
the pushing in the lunchline,
the papers turned in with no name,
the tattletales,
the whining,
the skinned knees,
the runny noses . . .

There's a starling
perched on the wire outside the window,
and I'd dearly love to trade places with him.
I understand more clearly than ever
mankind's yearning to fly.
Oh, to swoop away from all this!

Father, I can't fly away,
but I can be still.
I can be still and know that you are God.
You have called me to serve you as a teacher,
and while no one ever said teaching
was going to be easy,
you have promised to renew my strength.

I am envying a starling
when I could mount up with wings as an eagle:
"But they that wait upon the Lord
shall renew their strength;
they shall mount up with wings as eagles;
they shall run and not be weary;
they shall walk and not faint (Isa. 40:31).

For Help in Listening

Father,
even as I talk to you now,
I affirm my faith
that you are listening.
You have assured us
that before we cry, you will answer,
while we are yet speaking, you will hear.

Father,
I confess that there is freer access to the throne of grace
than there is to my desk.
I cherish the privilege
of being heard by the Lord of the universe,
yet I am careless about listening
to the children in my class.
I am like the irresponsible servant
who expected better treatment
than he was willing to give.

The children are so eager to talk to me,
but I am often harried and aloof
as I go frantically about the business of teaching.

I suspect I am missing the point.

How much I could learn about the children,
about teaching,
about myself,
if only I would take the time,
and make the effort
to listen.

Slow me down, Father.
Give me a heart that understands the importance
of a new pair of shoes
or a lost pencil.

If I have pressing matters at hand and must say,
"Not now, later,"
let me treat that as a solemn promise.

I expect the children to listen to me;
help me to listen to them.
Let me teach them by example
that one of the most generous and loving things
we can do for each other
is to "lend an ear."

So, Father,
forgive me my mistakes,
and strengthen me in my resolve to do better.
And, Father,
thank you for listening.

For the "Why-Aren't-I-Doing-Anything-Important?" Blues

Oh, Father,
How small this world of the classroom is,
bounded by alphabet charts and chalkboards,
bookcases and maps.

And how far this world seems
from the adult circles of money and prestige.
While other adults work together in those circles,
I am alone
among a throng of scurrying, chattering little people.

Little people and little things.
My days are so filled with little things.

Today I handed out a ream of kleenex,

marched a miscreant to the principal's office,
and put up a new bulletin board.

What am I doing here?
Why aren't I doing anything exciting and important
in the grownup world?

But, Father, there were *other* "little things" today.

Today Kevin came up to me,
bubbling with excitement,
and said,
"I can read this whole book all by myself!"

Today Michelle wrote a story that said:
"My dog is brown and white. He is a very nice person."

Today Kathleen,
who has hardly said two words all year,
raised her hand to answer a question.

Perhaps years from now
I'll learn the results of these "little things"
that happened today.
Perhaps I won't.
But, Father, teach me to take delight in little things,
and never, never let me doubt their importance.

For Self-Acceptance

F ather,
sometimes I think it might be easier
if she weren't in the classroom next door.
But then I think, No,

I'd still see her at the ditto machine,
neatly running off and slipping into file folders
math papers she will need,
not in fifteen minutes,
but in three weeks.

I'd still see her in the lounge,
sipping a diet soft drink,
as she reads Piaget for fun.

I'd still see her
drifting perfumed and polished down the hall,
stopping only to tell a seven-foot-tall kid
to scrape his gum out of the drinking fountain—
and being obeyed.

But, oh—
first thing in the morning it *is* hard
to have her right next door.
Hard,
to come skidding down the hall,
the purple ditto ink not yet dry on my nose,
and see her standing at her door
smiling serenely at her children as they arrive.
Smiling at her children.
First thing in the morning.

Oh, Father,
why can't I be like that?
You know, calm,
well-organized,
cheerful,
perfect?

I guess perfection's not my style.
You've helped me accept myself as a person—
imperfections and all.
So help me to accept myself as a teacher—
imperfections and all. Amen.

For Perspective

Father,
sometimes I think back to the video tapes
we saw in teacher training courses,
and I wonder what a tape of *my* classroom would show.

On some days, Father,
when I'm creative and energetic,
I think, "Let those cameras roll!"
Let them see a teacher
who drags out the brightly colored rods for a math
    lesson
instead of scribbling sketches on the board.
Let them see a teacher
who copes good humoredly
with children who eat paste.

That's on some days, Father.

On other days,
when I'm tired and at loose ends,
I shudder to think of anyone seeing me.
What a picture that would be, Lord.

There I am,
flapping my arms and screeching,
"Quiet, quiet, quiet!
Can't you children show a little SELF-CONTROL?!"

> *"O wad some Power the giftie gie us,*
> *To see oursels as ithers see us."*

But, "Thou, Lord, seest me."
You see me on the good days
and on the bad.
You know far more about my classroom
than a tape could ever show,
and you see me far more clearly

than I could *ever see* myself.
Yet, through it all,
inexplicably,
you go on loving me.
My good days have not earned your love,
and my bad days cannot diminish it.
Day by day, you go on loving me.

Lord,
help me to see myself more as you see me.
Help me to see the pattern of my days,
so that I am not puffed up by success
or cast down by failure.
Give me a sure and steady perspective.
Help me to know myself,
with all my strengths and weaknesses,
and with that knowledge, Father,
help me to grow.

For Confidence

Father,
I have this idea for something new.
(It's not in the Manual or anything;
it's just something I thought up myself.)
And I really think it might work.
It's just that I've never done
anything like it before.
Oh, I don't know.
Maybe I'd better not try it.
What do you think?

Yes, I *know* you've blessed me with
training, intelligence,
and drive.

It's just that
this idea I have—
well, it's not in the Manual or anything—
and it might flop. . . .

Excuse me a moment, Father,
while I dig my hole a little deeper.
It's for this measly little talent.
Goodness knows, I don't have many,
and I want to be sure the one I have
is buried deep and safe. . . .

For Consistency

Father, you who are the same
yesterday,
today,
and forever,
help me to be consistent.

Help me to make my classroom a secure and stable
    place,
where the children know what I expect of them;
and what they can expect from me.

I pray that it might be said of my classroom that

> nothing was ever promised that was not given,
> nothing was ever threatened that was not
>   carried out,
> nothing was ever said that was not true,
> nothing was ever taught that had to be
>   unlearned. *

*adapted from John Ruskin's
reflections upon his home.

For the Substitute

Well, Father,
here I am,
laid low with the flu,
and my thoughts are with my sub.

I have a few requests—
a sort of Substitute's Checklist,
because I've been there, Father, and I *know*.

☐ Please let her find the school.
It's in one of those new subdivisions
where hapless strangers have been known
to wander in,
valiantly searching for Pendragon Place,
never to return.

☐ Please banish from her thoughts
all memories of substituting stories
she has heard,
all tales of cherry bombs flushed down toilets,
wastepaper baskets set on fire,
chairs tossed from second-story windows.
It does no good to dwell on that.

☐ Please let her see on my desk
the names of the two most reliable kids—
the *only* two reliable kids—
I chose to be her "Helpers for the Day."
And please don't let them both have chicken pox.

☐ Please let her find the ladies' room.
(This is second only to finding the school.)

☐ Please give her a keen sense of judgment
when Billy says,
"My brother must have gotten my homework
mixed up with his.

May I go up to Mr. Whitaker's class
and get it, please?"
Billy has no brother.
And there is no Mr. Whitaker.

☐ And for the children, Father,
please give them the will to do their very best,
to treat the sub as if she were a welcome friend.
And gently bring to their minds
all I said I'd do to them
if I find their names
on a list
when I return.

In Praise of Books

Today the children responded with open delight
as I read them a story
which was written over one hundred fifty years ago
and half a world away.
A story which was read to me
when I was their age,
every night,
upon demand.

And now it is their turn, Father,
to receive this story in joy,
and claim it for their own.

What a marvel language is,
that it can freeze an author's thoughts and emotions,
and preserve them,
until they melt into the mind and heart
of a reader.

What a wonder words are,
that they can transcend space and time,
class and race,

uniting your sons and daughters
in literary fellowship.

Father, thank you for books.
Thank you for children.
And thank you for the delightful privilege
of bringing the two together.

In Praise of Learning

For reading;
that peculiar marks on a page are so able to inform us,
to entertain us,
and move us to laughter and tears,
we thank you, Father.

For handwriting, grammar and spelling;
which as tools enable us to capture our thoughts
and communicate them clearly to others,
we thank you, Father.

For mathematics;
with its dependable patterns and principles
which reassure us that the world is not so inconstant
as we might fear,
we thank you, Father.

For science;
which challenges us to explore our universe
and reveals the world to be all the more wonderful
the more we understand it,
we thank you, Father.

For social studies;
which teaches us to know ourselves
and to know each other,
we thank you, Father.

For art;
with its absorbing, unexcelled joy
of making,
seeing, and appreciating the beautiful,
we thank you, Father.

For music;
with its mystical power to reach us
and unite us
as nothing else can,
we thank you, Father.

For physical education;
which teaches us to understand our bodies,
and gain satisfaction inherent in strength and skill,
we thank you, Father.

Father,
for all truth,
and for hearts and minds to know the truth,
we thank you.

For the Parent-Teacher Conference

We're both a little defensive, Father,
as we face each other across the desk.
I'm worried about what I'll say;
she's worried about what she'll hear;
and we're both worried about what the other is thinking.

Father, let her think kindly of me.
While she has primary responsibility for her child,
help her to know that he's very important to me, too.
In a sense, children belong to all of us,
and I invest a great deal of time, effort, and skill
in teaching the child who comes to me.

Father, let me think kindly of her.
Teach me how to know the difference between concern
    and nosiness.
Keep me from sitting in judgment—
automatically blaming her for her child's problems;
benevolently bestowing my advice.
Remind me that, while I have to cope with him for six
    hours a day,
she has to live with him.

We're both a little defensive, Father, so ease the tension.
Give us the problem-solving strength
    that comes from working together.

For the Teacher Next Year

Father,
in her uncompromising scales I am weighed,
and, inevitably,
found wanting.

She says,
"Of course, the work I'm doing now
is work they should have gotten last year.
These children come to me knowing nothing."

I hasten to assure myself,
"That's not true."
But Father,
her arrow-sharp remarks
find their way home
to my insecurities and doubts
and cause more pain that I care to admit.

Father, if there's some truth in what she says,
help me to heed it.

If not,
help me to ignore it.
Relieve me of the anxiety and bitterness
this teacher's criticism brings.
Keep me from becoming petty and vindictive.
And do not let my defenses against unfair criticism
make me proud and unbending,
so that I cannot learn and grow.

Father, before you,
I am doing the best job I can.
Let me take comfort in that.
Amid the stress and conflict of life,
I have your firm and loving exhortation:
Fret not.
So help me to put my fretting aside
and get on with the work you have given me to do.

And when another teacher sends her children up to me,
help me to remember
how much criticism hurts.

On Showing Love

I found a note on the floor this afternoon, Father.
The children,
giddy with their newfound power over the written word,
have been ecstatically scribbling love notes
to each other
and to me.

I found a note on the floor this afternoon, Father;
this one's addressed to you:

> *Dear God,*
> *I love you.*

Do you love me?
Check one
YES □ *or NO* □

I smile at the request, but then,
oh, Father!
A sudden joy
wells up within me,
almost choking me
with its intensity,
when I think how abundantly
you have already checked, YES.
Checked our timid little question boxes
With your searing stroke of love.

Our loving Father.
Our matchless God.
For you exist—
and that would have been enough.
For you create—
and that would have been enough.
For you sustain—
and that would have been enough.
But that you should *love*!

Oh, God,
the heart of man cannot contain
the engulfing wonder of your love.

So let me not question
but receive.

Let your love well up within me.
Let it well up and spill over,
assuring the little one who wrote the note
and all who hunger in their hearts to know,
that the answer is Yes.

The answer is Yes.